Caravan and Holiday Cookery

Jean Smith

Published by Sigma Leisure - an imprint of
Sigma Press, 1 South Oak Lane, Wilmslow, Cheshire SK9 6AR, England.

British Library Cataloguing in Publication Data
A CIP record for this book is available from the British Library.

ISBN: 1-85058-557-1

Editorial, typesetting and page design by: Sigma Press, Wilmslow, Cheshire.

Cover photograph: Philip Pickard Photography, Birmingham

Cover design and printing: MFP Design & Print

Illustrations: Vanessa Betts

Contents

Introduction

Holiday time. A time to relax, see new sights, recharge your batteries. A time to leave household chores behind, to be happy and enjoy family life. Or are your holidays more like this . . .

To get away from chores, you eat ready-made meals and canned foods. This rapidly becomes boring and leads to complaints from the family – no disrespect to the food canners, but eating canned carrots, although highly nutritious, twice in one week is definitely beyond the call of duty. So you decide to eat out. The younger members of the family want burger and chips, you want a 'decent' meal, so you end up with family squabbles. The food isn't cooked the way you like it, the portion sizes are wrong. More grumbles from the family. You end up cooking the same meals that you would at home, which you didn't really want to do, and all the family spend more time in the holiday accommodation, waiting for meals to be cooked.

If any of the above sounds familiar, take heart. There is another alternative: it is possible, by cooking simply and using ready-made items imaginatively, to produce meals which are tasty, nutritious and take less time to prepare, cook and clean up after than you might spend waiting in a queue for fish and chips. It is this alternative that this book addresses, but don't relegate it to holidays only – many of these recipes are also firm favourites at home, and a boon in our sometimes busy and often chaotic household.

Many meals in this book are so quick and easy that all members of the family can take their turn in the kitchen, even the children, making it easier to share tasks while on holiday. Many of the desserts are particularly easy to create.

The meals have been developed over many years of caravanning and motorcaravanning. Some were carefully thought out, some inspirational, and even some desperational, but all share one aspect: they can all be cooked on two rings and a grill, using a minimum of utensils.

You will need a minimum of one saucepan for the recipes, but two would be preferable. Additionally, you will need two frying pans one large, one small. A set of small plastic measuring spoons and plastic measuring jug will also be required. Don't forget something to stir with, it beats burning your fingers every time!

The secret is to carry a limited stock of dried herbs, spices and flavourings. These help to replace flavour which is lost during drying, canning or otherwise preserving the food. The minimum list of such items would be:

Salt
Parsley
Black Peppercorns in a mill or coarsely ground
Herbes de Provence (or mixed herbs)
Cayenne Pepper or Chilli Powder
Curry Powder
Ground Ginger
Stock Cubes (beef, chicken and vegetable)
Paprika
Garlic Purée

This collection won't take up much room, and the space can further be cut down by using a multi-compartment container for the dry spices and herbs.

Additional items you may like to carry:

Mint Sauce
Mustard
Garlic Salt
Herb Oils; especially rosemary, bay and garlic.
Ground Cumin
Ground Coriander
Celery Salt

Dips, Appetizers and Salads

Cottage Cheese Dip

227g carton cottage cheese
½ tsp dried parsley
1 sachet instant golden vegetable soup

Mix all the ingredients in a small bowl. Serve well chilled.

Crab Dip

43 g can dressed crab
1 tablespoon mayonnaise
1 teaspoon lemon juice

Mix all the ingredients in a small bowl. Serve well chilled.

Chilli Dip

1 tablespoon tomato ketchup
1 tablespoon brown sauce
¼ teaspoon chilli pepper

Mix all the ingredients. Add more chilli if you like your sauce hotter. Serve well chilled.

Mushroom Dip

1 can creamed mushrooms
4 cm (2 in) garlic purée
1 tablespoon mayonnaise
1 teaspoon lemon juice

Mix all the ingredients. Serve well chilled.

Chicken and Crab Cocktail

2 large leaves from an iceberg lettuce
shredded lettuce leaves
43g can dressed crab
2 slices chicken roll

Place the iceberg lettuce leaves into bowls. Spread each piece of chicken roll thickly with dressed crab and put inside a lettuce leaf. Loosely fill with shredded lettuce. Make up Marie Rose sauce (see page 66) by mixing equal quantities of salad cream and ketchup, then spoon into leaf.

Devilled Mushrooms

300 g can sliced mushrooms
shredded lettuce
1 tablespoon oil for frying
150 g (6 oz) medium onion (chopped)
pinch cayenne pepper
2 teaspoons Worcester sauce
1 level tablespoon tomato purée
2 cm (1 in) Garlic purée

Heat oil in frying pan, add the onion and cook gently for approximately 2 minutes. Stir in the Worcester sauce, the garlic and tomato purées and add cayenne pepper to taste. Drain the mushrooms, add them to the frying pan and heat through. Place the shredded lettuce in bottom of a glass dish and cover with the mushroom mixture. Serve immediately.

Stuffed Mushrooms

7 small button mushrooms per person
125 g (5 oz) packet of cream cheese (any variety)
1 large (4 – 6 servings) packet of instant mash
1 size 3 egg
2 tablespoons sunflower oil
dried parsley

Remove stalks from the mushrooms. Spoon the cream cheese into the mushroom cups. Add parsley to instant mash and make up as per instructions. Allow to cool, then add egg and mix well. Coat each mushroom in the potato mixture. Heat oil until very hot, then fry mushrooms turning carefully until golden brown. Serve with a side salad.

Prawn & Mango Cocktail

4 tablespoons mayonnaise
1 teaspoon tomato ketchup
1 medium mango
100 g (4 oz) prawns (tinned and drained or frozen defrosted)
shredded lettuce leaves
1 pinch paprika
1 slice lemon (optional)

Peel and dice the mango. Blend together the mayonnaise and tomato ketchup. Coat the mango and prawns with mixture. Put lettuce leaves into the bottom of 4 serving bowls. Place the mixture on top. Garnish with lemon slice and pinch of paprika.

Prawn Cocktail

200 g can prawns
1 iceberg lettuce
Marie Rose sauce (see page 66)
slices of lemon for garnish (optional)

Drain the prawns and reserve a few for garnish. Shred the iceberg lettuce. Add prawns to sauce and mix until coated. Place lettuce in the bottom of glasses and spoon sauce over the top. Garnish with reserved prawns and slice of lemon.

Kedgeree

1 smoked haddock fillet
3 size 3 eggs
25 g (1 oz) butter
75 g (3 oz) long grain rice
1 teaspoon dried parsley

Hard boil 2 eggs, remove their shells, chop one and slice the other. Cook the rice for 15 minutes in boiling salted water. Cook the haddock in simmering water for 10 minutes then drain. Break into pieces with a fork. Melt the butter in a saucepan; add parsley, rice and fish, stirring with a fork until hot. Mix in the chopped eggs and seasonings. Beat the third egg and stir in. When the mixture is creamy, serve hot, garnished with sliced egg and a sprinkle of fresh parsley if available.

Potato and Frankfurter Terrine

1 large (4-6 servings) packet instant mash
400 g (drained 184g) can frankfurters or cocktail sausages
1 heaped teaspoon mild curry powder
1 size 3 egg

Drain sausages, then chop roughly. Add curry powder to mashed potato powder and make up according to the instant mash instructions. Add egg and mix quickly. Add the chopped sausages to the potato and mix well. Put in a dish, press down, then chill. Serve with grapefruit salad (see page 9).

Salmon Terrine

240 g can red salmon

425 g can processed peas

50 g (2 oz) butter or margarine

ground black pepper

Drain the salmon, remove skin and bones. Flake fish. Drain the peas and mash roughly. Combine salmon and peas then season with pepper. Melt the butter and pour into salmon/pea mix and stir through. Put into small dish and press down. Chill thoroughly. Serve with fingers of toast and garnish with fresh watercress if available.

Mackerel Terrine

125 g can mackerel in brine

425 g can processed peas

300 g can button mushrooms

50 g (2 oz) butter or margarine

ground black pepper

Drain the mackerel, then remove the skin and bones. Flake fish. Drain peas and mash roughly. Finely slice the mushrooms and combine with the mackerel and peas, stir through. Melt butter and pour into mackerel/pea/mushroom mix and combine together. Put into small dish and press down. Chill thoroughly. Serve with fingers of toast and garnish with fresh watercress if available.

Tuna and Cream Cheese pate

213g can tuna (drained)

100 g (4 oz) cream cheese

2 teaspoons lemon juice

½ teaspoon paprika

Flake the tuna and combine with cream cheese and lemon juice. Sprinkle with paprika. Serve with toast.

Grapefruit Salad

½ 284g can grapefruit segments

strips of crispy fried bacon

1 Lollo Rossa lettuce

Clean lettuce. Drain grapefruit segments. Arrange leaves and grapefruit alternately on a plate or dish, then sprinkle with bacon strips. Serve with Potato and Frankfurter Terrine (see page 7).

Hot Pasta Salad

200 g (8 oz) pasta shapes
226g small can chopped tomatoes or roughly chopped plum tomatoes
1 teaspoon Herbes de Provence
1 tablespoon olive oil
1 tablespoon mayonnaise

Cook pasta according to instructions, then drain. Into the saucepan put the other ingredients except for the mayonnaise and heat gently. Return the pasta to the pan, stir and reheat until the pasta is coated with sauce. At the last minute add the mayonnaise and stir. Serve immediately with meat of your choice.

Olive Salad

2 tomatoes
salt and pepper
4 black olives (pitted)
4 green olives (pitted)
1 level teaspoon dried basil

Slice the tomatoes and sprinkle with salt and pepper. Add the olives and toss lightly. Sprinkle with basil.

Vegetables

Most vegetables used, with the exception of onions and mushrooms, are from cans. Although superb nutritionally, they don't always taste their best, hence the recipes. Almost all vegetables can be bought in canned form. I have even seen canned Brussels Sprouts, but never had the courage to try them!

A note about Instant Mash; even the best brands can taste less than acceptable after one serving. However, it is easily incorporated into other dishes where the taste is modified and thereby becomes acceptable. Instant Mash is excellent for thickening soups, stews and sauces. Just sprinkle it directly into the hot liquid and stir. Keep adding until you reach the desired consistency. Any lumps will disappear if you keep stirring gently. The sauce in Orange Minted Potatoes can be thickened this way.

Refried Beans

410 g can red kidney beans, drained

2 rashers streaky bacon, chopped

¼ teaspoon salt

⅛ teaspoon cayenne or chilli pepper

grated Parmesan cheese

Fry the bacon until tender. Mash the beans with salt and pepper. Add to the bacon and fry until brown. Sprinkle with grated Parmesan cheese.

Carrot & Apple Medley

I created this recipe when I wanted vegetables to accompany pork chops and only had one saucepan left – so I cooked everything in the same saucepan.

1 medium onion

300 g can sliced carrots

1 medium apple

Coarsely chop or slice the onion and fry gently in a little olive oil or butter. Peel and slice the apple, add to the onions and continue to cook until the apple softens. Drain the carrots, then add them to the mixture and stir gently until the carrots are heated through. Garnish with fresh herbs or sesame seeds; use as an accompaniment to pork chops, chicken portions or sausages.

Haricot Vert à Bias

283g can cut green beans
25 g (1 oz) butter
2 cm (1 in) garlic purée

Drain the beans. Put the butter and garlic purée in a small saucepan and melt the butter. Add the beans, stirring gently until heated through and evenly coated with butter and garlic.

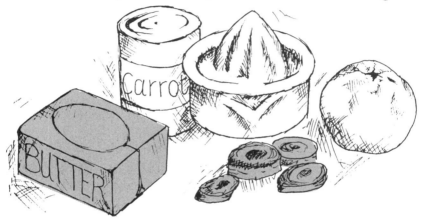

Honeyed Carrots

300 g can sliced carrots

25 g (1 oz) butter

1 teaspoon orange juice

1 dessertspoon honey or brown sugar

2 teaspoons dried parsley

Drain the carrots and place in a saucepan. Add the orange juice, parsley and honey (or brown sugar) and mix well; simmer gently for five minutes. Drain, reserving juice. Thicken the juice with instant potato powder and serve as a sauce.

Sesame Carrots

300 g can whole carrots

1 teaspoon sesame seeds

Toast the sesame seeds by heating in a dry pan; drop in seeds and stir quickly over a high heat. Heat the canned carrots, then drain and sprinkle with toasted sesame seeds.

Carrot Stuffing

Vegetable and accompaniment in one easy recipe!

300 g can sliced carrots

½ packet sage & onion stuffing

Drain the carrots, reserving juice, and mash the carrots in a bowl. Add the stuffing mixture and mix thoroughly. Heat the carrot juice and add to the mixture; stir well. Leave for fifteen minutes. Stir again then shape into balls or patties. Grill in a lightly greased grill pan with the rack removed or shallow fry. Excellent with all cooked meats.

Variation: try different flavoured stuffing mixes.

Country Mash

1 packet (4-6 servings) instant mashed potato

2 sachets golden vegetable cupasoup (without croûtons)

Mix the dry powders together in a bowl. Add boiling water, using ¼ pint more than instructions on the mash packet. Stir until thickened. Serve as you would mashed potato.

Creamed Potatoes

1 packet (4-6 servings) instant mashed potato
2 tablespoons instant milk

Mix dry powders and make up as plain mashed potato. Serve with knobs of butter.

Curried Bubble

425 g can macedoine (mixed diced vegetables)
2 teaspoons curry powder
1 packet (4-6 servings) instant mashed potato
1 size 3 egg

Add the curry powder to dry instant mashed potato and then make up according to the instructions. Add the egg, then mix until evenly distributed. Drain the mixed vegetables and add to the curried potato. Fry in a little oil until browned. Serve with a mixed grill or a fry up.

Orange Minted Potatoes

560 g can new potatoes
½ teaspoon mint sauce
1 cup pure orange juice
1 tablespoon instant mashed potato

Drain the canned potatoes. Mix mint and orange juice, pour over the potatoes. Heat gently for 5-6 minutes. Lift out the potatoes. Thicken the orange/mint liquid with instant mashed potato and serve as a sauce.

Parmajano Patties

1 packet (4-6 servings) instant mashed potato
1 heaped tablespoon grated Parmesan
50 g packet chopped mixed nuts
1 size 3 egg

Make up the instant mash according to the instructions. Add the egg, Parmesan and nuts. Shape into patties and fry in a little oil until browned on both sides. Serve with mixed vegetables or salad.

Potatoes in Sour Cream

560 g can new potatoes

125ml carton sour cream (or fresh cream with a few drops of lemon juice)

1 teaspoon dried parsley

Heat potatoes, adding lemon juice and parsley to liquor. Drain, then add sour cream and reheat gently. Serve with cooked meats or salad.

Quick Lyonnaise Potatoes

560 g can potatoes

1 tablespoon sunflower oil

1 medium onion

Peel and slice the onions and gently fry in the oil until transparent. Cut the potatoes into slices and add to the onions. Turn up the heat and cook until onions and potatoes are golden.

Pasta and Rice

I make no apologies for including so many pasta and rice recipes; dried pasta and rice are perfect convenience foods for the person with limited space. They need no special storage, no preparation and are extremely versatile and nutritious. Incidentally, pasta and rice can be interchanged in most recipes. Couscous is a North African staple food which is made from Durum wheat. Being pre-cooked it is very easy to use; you will find it at large supermarkets and 'ethnic' grocers.

Beef and Mushroom Pasta

295 g can condensed mushroom soup
2 slices cooked beef
250 g (10 oz) pasta shapes

Cut the beef into strips. Cook the pasta in water without salt. Heat the soup without adding any water, stir in the beef. Drain the pasta and toss in the sauce. Serve with a side salad.

Other combinations: Chicken soup and fresh or canned mushrooms; Asparagus soup and boiled ham or salami.

Creamy Mushroom Pasta

250 g (10 oz) pasta shapes
295 g can condensed cream of mushroom soup
2 size 3 hard boiled eggs
340 g (12 oz) frozen mixed vegetables

Cook the pasta in boiling water for ten minutes, then add the packet of vegetables. Cook for a further three to four minutes. Drain. Add the soup without any additional water. Reheat gently.
Serve with roughly chopped hard boiled eggs sprinkled over the top.

Cream Cheese Pasta

250 g (10 oz) pasta shapes
125 g Philadelphia soft cheese with chives
75 g (3 oz) boiled ham
227g can pineapple chunks
garlic salt

Cook pasta in water seasoned with garlic salt. Cut the ham into strips. Melt the cream cheese slowly, stir in the ham and pineapple, including juice. Drain the pasta and toss in sauce. Sprinkle with Parmesan cheese. Serve with a salad if desired.

Creamy Chicken Pasta

250 g (10 oz) pasta shapes
295 g can condensed cream of chicken soup
100 g (4 oz) chicken roll
340 g (12 oz) packet frozen mixed vegetables

Cook pasta in boiling water for ten minutes. Add the packet of vegetables and cook for further three to four minutes. Cut the chicken roll into strips. Drain pasta and vegetables, add to the soup without any additional water. Reheat gently, adding chicken strips at the last minute. Serve immediately.

Mediterranean Medley

1 can chopped tomatoes and herbs
250 g (10 oz) pasta shapes
2 cabanos
1 teaspoon olive oil
Grated Parmesan cheese

Cook pasta in boiling salted water, drain. Add chopped tomatoes, olive oil and chopped cabanos. Stir and reheat. Serve with grated Parmesan cheese.

Couscous

500 g (1lb) couscous medium pre-cooked

500ml (1pt) water

knob of butter

Add water to couscous in a saucepan and let it soak for 10 minutes. Heat over a low heat, adding butter and stirring constantly. Serve hot with a sauce or cold with salad.

Variation: add 1 teaspoon of lemon juice and 1 tablespoon of sultanas at the soaking stage. When almost heated add 50 g (2 oz) shelled pistachio nuts or 50 g (2 oz) flaked almonds.

Pasta Alfredo

200 g (8 oz) pasta

75 g (3 oz) grated Parmesan cheese

125ml (¼ pint) double cream

1 level teaspoon dried parsley

salt and pepper

Place butter and cream in a pan, stir over low heat until butter is melted and combined with the cream. Remove from heat, add cheese, parsley, salt and pepper then stir until the sauce is blended and smooth. Meanwhile, cook the pasta, drain, then place in a pan with the sauce and toss until evenly coated. Serve immediately with salad.

Pasta Parisian

184g can or 150 g (6 oz) lunch tongue
200 g (8 oz) pasta twists
5 cm (2 in) garlic purée
200ml (⅓ pint) crème fraiche
1 heaped teaspoon dried basil
knob of butter
1 tablespoon olive oil
Salt and pepper

Cook the pasta in boiling, salted water until tender. While the pasta is cooking, melt the butter in another saucepan. Add basil and garlic to the butter and stir over moderate heat for one minute. Stir in crème fraiche and season to taste. Bring to the boil then simmer gently. Cut the tongue into strips. Drain the pasta. Into the pasta saucepan put the olive oil and tongue and fry gently for thirty seconds. Return the pasta to the pan and stir over a gentle heat until tongue is mixed in.

Seafood Pasta

200 g (8 oz) pasta shells

43g can dressed crab

2 cm (1 in) vegetable purée (tube)

200 g can prawns

6 black olives (de-stoned & cut into quarters)

2 heaped tablespoons dried milk.

Drain the prawns and use the liquor to make up dried milk. Add the vegetable purée and dressed crab to the milk mixture to make up a sauce. Cook the pasta shells and drain thoroughly. Put a small amount of oil in a pan and heat gently. Place pasta in the pan and toss. Add the sauce and continue tossing over a gentle heat until the shells are evenly coated. Add the prawns and olives; toss, then serve at once on warmed plates.

Spaghetti Campolina

200 g (8 oz) spaghetti

205 g small can minced meat

1 tin chopped tomatoes with herbs

Cook spaghetti in boiling water. Meanwhile mix minced meat and chopped tomatoes together. Heat gently. When spaghetti is cooked drain and pour sauce over coating evenly. Serve with grated Parmesan cheese.

Spaghetti Carbonara

200 g (8 oz) spaghetti
50 g (2 oz) boiled ham or prawns
4 tablespoons dried milk
2 size 3 eggs
2 tablespoons water
1 heaped teaspoon dried parsley
1 tablespoon grated Parmesan cheese

Cook the pasta. Meanwhile, mix eggs, water, dried milk and parsley. Beat well. Cut the ham into strips. Drain pasta. Put oil into pan, heat gently. Put in the pasta and toss over gentle heat, then pour in the sauce slowly and mix thoroughly, do not over cook. Add the ham, mix in. Serve immediately.

Spaghetti Neapolitan

200 g (8 oz) spaghetti
397g can chopped plum tomatoes
1 level teaspoon dried basil
2 cm (1 in) garlic purée
1 teaspoon sugar
2 tablespoons olive oil
Salt & pepper
Parmesan cheese

Heat 1 tablespoon of olive oil in the large sauce pan, put in the tomatoes, garlic purée, herbs, sugar, salt & pepper. Cook over medium heat for 10 minutes stirring occasionally. Cook the spaghetti according to instructions, drain and return to pan with 1 tablespoon of olive oil. Toss the spaghetti until coated with oil. Add the sauce to pan and toss again. Serve topped with Parmesan cheese.

Creamed Crab Pilaff

200 g (8 oz) long grain rice
25 g (1 oz) peas
170 g can white crab meat
100 g (4 oz) double cream
1 chicken stock cube
1 level teaspoon dried parsley

Cook the rice in water, crab brine and stock cube until all liquid is absorbed, Add peas and crab meat. Reheat gently, stirring all the time. Add the cream and parsley. Reheat gently and serve immediately.

Prawn and Banana Curry

1 carton or can curry sauce (preferably korma)
200 g can prawns
1 large banana
4 teaspoons powdered milk or coffee whitener

Drain excess brine from prawns. Place sauce, prawns and sliced banana in saucepan and heat gently, stirring occasionally. Sprinkle with powdered milk and mix. Serve immediately on a bed of rice.

Variation: fresh prawns or chopped crabsticks can be substituted for canned prawns.

Spicy Risotto

200 g (8 oz) easy cook rice

425 g can spicy chicken and vegetable soup

218g can salmon or 185 g can tuna

Put rice in the pan and pour in soup. Cook rice in the soup adding more water if necessary. When the rice is cooked (about fifteen minutes) and all the water is absorbed, add flaked fish, mix over gentle heat. Serve garnished with side salad.

Vegetable Rice

1 mug long grain rice

½ teaspoon dried parsley

425 g can mixed vegetables

Cook the rice in water with parsley. When almost cooked, add the vegetables and reheat. Serve with Creamed Sweetcorn and Prawns (page 59).

Chilli Beans

The small brown sign indicated there was a picnic site '3' something away. Navigation in the Republic of Ireland is always a bit hit and miss; the Government is changing the road signs from miles to kilometres. This is being accomplished on a haphazard basis and there is a mixture of measurements on signs with no indication as to which is which. Sometimes, when EU grants are received, a kilometre or two of beautiful dual carriageway is built, often in the middle of nowhere, obliterating picnic sites, but the signs indicating its presence still remain. It took us two hours of driving in circles to find our picnic site, religiously following the brown signs; it was only when, in the fading light, we turned down an unposted side road and then drove past the unmarked entrance were we able to stop for the evening. No-one was in any mood to fuss over cooking and we were all as ravenous as wolves; out of desperation 'Chilli Beans' was born.

   400 g can peeled plum tomatoes
   410 g can red kidney beans
   2 vegetable stock cubes
   1 teaspoon tomato purée
   1 teaspoon garlic purée or 2 cloves crushed garlic
   ¼ teaspoon chilli or cayenne pepper
   Seasoning to taste

Empty the tomatoes into saucepan and mash with wooden spoon. Drain the kidney beans and add to the tomatoes. Crumble stock cubes into saucepan; if they are the sort that don't crumble, then add the cube and stir over a gentle heat until dissolved. Add pepper, tomato and garlic purée, stir gently to mix. Simmer gently for seven minutes. Serve over cooked pasta or rice. Garnish with Parmesan Cheese or grated Cheddar Cheese.

Main Meals

Most main meal recipes are meat based but in recent years I have experimented more with vegetarian meals; they are generally lower fat, lower calorie, easier to cook and usually, very tasty: well worth investigation!

Corned Beef and Cabbage

340 g can corned beef

50 g (2 oz) butter or margarine

1 small or ½ large white cabbage

Salt and pepper to taste

Shred the cabbage and plunge into lightly salted boiling water. Bring back to the boil and cook for 7 to 10 minutes. Meanwhile cut the corned beef into small cubes. Drain the cooked cabbage thoroughly. In the same saucepan gently melt the butter. Put in the cabbage, corned beef and seasoning. Stir or toss over a low heat for 45 seconds. Serve on its own or with boiled potatoes for outdoor appetites!

Cheesy Main Course Soup

100 g (4 oz) strong Cheddar cheese grated

2 medium potatoes peeled and diced

or

425 g small can mixed vegetables

100 g (4 oz) spaghetti

1 large teaspoon tomato purée

$\frac{1}{2}$ teaspoon dried basil

1 rasher of middle cut bacon sliced very small

3 vegetable stock cubes

Make up a stock in a large saucepan. Mix in the tomato purée and basil. Add the rice, spaghetti, potatoes and bacon. Simmer for 12 minutes. Serve in large bowls with grated cheese piled on top.

Aylesbury Patties

8 x 50 g (2 oz) beef burgers (frozen defrosted)

295 g can duck with orange soup

50 g (2 oz) button mushrooms

Oil for frying

Heat the oil and fry the burgers until brown on both sides. Add the mushrooms and fry for further 1-2 minutes. Drain off oil and pour soup over burgers. Simmer for 10 minutes. Serve with creamed potatoes.

Creamy Gammon

4 slices of gammon
125ml (¼pint) double cream
1 teaspoon dried parsley
225 g can pineapple chunks

Drain the pineapple. (Save the juice to use in a cocktail if liked.) Cook gammon under the grill or fry. In a small saucepan, gently heat cream with dried parsley. Just before serving add the pineapple chunks and heat through. Place the gammon slices on plates and cover with sauce.

Beef Quickenuff

150200 g (6-8 oz) fillet steak
100 g (4 oz) button mushrooms
150ml (6fl oz) double cream
1 teaspoon dried parsley
oil for frying
garlic salt

Cut fillet into strips and fry quickly for 2 minutes. Add whole button mushrooms and cook for further 2 minutes. Mix cream, parsley and garlic salt, pour over beef. Reduce heat and cook gently without boiling to reduce liquid. Season to taste. Serve with salad or vegetables.

Beef Rolls with Blue Cheese

Tartex is a Swiss vegetarian 'pate' that comes in a tube and has long keeping properties; it also tastes excellent.

6 slices cooked beef

mushroom or herb Tartex

75 g (3 oz) blue cheese (preferably Stilton), crumbled

Spread each slice of beef with the Tartex and roll up, securing with a cocktail stick if necessary. Place in grill pan with wire rack removed. Place under grill and heat gently for 8-10 minutes. Remove and sprinkle with crumbled cheese. Replace under grill and continue cooking until cheese has melted. Serve immediately with plain vegetables.

Beef Somerset

200 g (8 oz) fillet steak

2 tablespoons cider vinegar

50 g (2 oz) butter

Ground black pepper

2 tablespoons apple juice

Cut the fillet steak into strips. Melt the butter in pan and allow to brown. Add pepper. Quickly fry the steak, turning to cook evenly. Add the apple juice and then evaporate over high heat. Add vinegar and evaporate as before. Serve garnished with fresh parsley if available and rice or boiled potatoes.

Dijon Beef

198g can cured chopped beef & ham

170 g small can sterilised cream + 1 teaspoon lemon juice or 120 g crème fraiche

cayenne pepper

1 rounded teaspoon Dijon mustard

Cut the meat into strips. Mix the cream, mustard and lemon juice (or mustard and crème fraiche). Combine the meat with the sauce. Serve with a tiny sprinkle of cayenne pepper and Olive Salad (page 10).

Steak Paprikash

2 x 200 g (8 oz) sirloin steaks

3 teaspoons paprika

garlic oil

Rub each steak with paprika at least 1 hour before required. Fry in olive oil to which a little garlic oil has been added. Serve with vegetables of your choice.

Steak with Cream Cheese and Pepper Sauce

200 g (8 oz) sirloin or fillet steak
125 g (5 oz) cream cheese
1 tablespoon oil
Freshly ground pepper

Fry the steak according to taste in the oil. Remove and keep warm. Melt cream cheese in frying pan and blend with oil and steak juices. Add ground pepper. Serve steak coated in sauce with extra pepper ground on top with new potatoes and salad.

Bacon Badger

100 g (4 oz) streaky bacon
1 tablespoon dried onion
500mls (1pt) water
375 g can butter beans
50 g (2 oz) white long grain rice

Fry bacon until tender. In a large pan place water, butter beans (including liquid), dried onion, rice and bacon (including fat). Simmer for ten minutes. Drain. Serve with side salad.

Bacon Chops with Ginger

1 packet bacon chops

125mls (1/4pint) ginger beer or dry ginger ale

Oil for frying

Single cream or substitute

Fry the chops in a little oil to seal and brown. Add ginger ale/beer and simmer gently for eight to ten minutes. Lift the chops out and place on plates. Add cream to pan and heat gently. Pour over chops.

Serve with the accompaniment of your choice.

Guinness Stir Fry

'In Dublin's Fair city' . . . well, as in any other city, there are some not-so-fair places, but under the influence of Dublin's most famous product, Guinness, the distinction blurs. Anyone who has only tasted Guinness in Mainland Britain cannot possibly appreciate the real thing. As you plunge into Guinness' crowning glory, thicker and sweeter than double cream, then taste the black velvet below. For some unknown reason, Guinness will not cross water without changing; the drink available in Mainland Britain is a thin and bitter shadow of the Irish version. Anyway, this recipe is an object lesson in the results of cooking under the influence whilst still imbibing;

it sometimes turns out better than the original, which did not have Guinness as one of its ingredients!

400 g (1lb) diced pork
125m ($\frac{1}{4}$ pint) Guinness
150 g (6 oz) mushrooms
1 tablespoon oil
1 packet stir fry vegetables
salt and pepper

Fry the diced pork in the oil until browned. Add the mush-rooms and cook quickly. Add the packet of vegetables, mix in and cook for about 30 seconds. Pour in the Guinness, add seasoning to taste and cook for a further 90 seconds. Serve with rice or noodles.

Turkey & Pepper Stir Fry

2 x 250-275 g (10-12 oz) turkey breast fillets
1 medium onion
1 green pepper
1 yellow pepper
1 heaped teaspoon cornflour
2 tablespoons soy sauce
oil for frying
salt

Cut the turkey into bite size pieces. Chop onion roughly. De-seed and chop the peppers. Mix cornflour and soy sauce. Fry turkey until lightly browned all over. Add onion and continue frying until the onion goes transparent. Add the peppers and fry for a further minute. Sprinkle with salt. Add cornflour and soy sauce mixture and stir quickly until thickened. Serve with rice or noodles.

Chilli Pork Stir Fry

250-275 g (10-12 oz) pork fillet

¼ teaspoon chilli pepper

½ teaspoon ground cumin

2 cm (1 in) garlic purée

300 g can button mushrooms

1 medium onion, chopped

2 tablespoons soy sauce

1 tablespoon sherry

150 g (6 oz) broccoli (fresh or frozen, defrosted)

2 teaspoons sugar

Slice the pork thinly. Put in a dish or plastic bag with sugar, chilli, cumin and garlic. Cover and leave for at least 30 minutes. Cut broccoli into small pieces. Drain the mushrooms. Heat a small amount of oil in the large frying pan. Add pork and stir fry for 5-6 minutes. Add the vegetables and cook for a further 2 minutes. Pour in liquids and cook for a further minute. Serve with rice or noodles.

Beef with Ginger Stir Fry

200 g (8 oz) beef fillet

1 medium onion, sliced or a bunch of spring onions chopped

2 cm (1 in) garlic purée

2 teaspoons sherry

1 level teaspoon ground ginger

4 fresh tomatoes, quartered

Cut the beef fillet into strips. Place in dish or plastic bag and sprinkle on ginger, leave for at least 30 minutes; then heat a little oil in the large frying pan. Add the beef and onions and stir fry for 2-3 minutes. Add the tomatoes and garlic purée and continue stir frying for a further 2 minutes. Add sherry and simmer for 1 minute. Serve with rice or noodles.

Chicken and Cashew Nut Stir Fry

250-300 g (10-12 oz) boneless chicken breast

100 g (4 oz) cashew nuts (roasted salted)

1 medium onion, chopped

1 vegetable stock cube

oil for frying

165ml (⅓ pint) water

Cut the chicken into bite size pieces. Quickly rinse the salted nuts. Fry the chicken in a little oil for 3-4 minutes. Add the onion and fry for a further 3 minutes. Sprinkle with the crumbled stock cube and add the nuts. Fry for a further minute. Add water and simmer for 1 minute.

Poulet Flandres

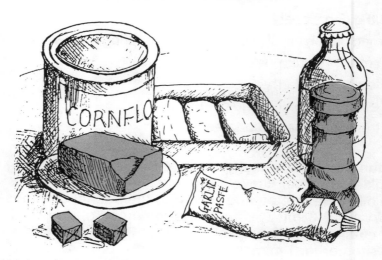

4 chicken breast portions

25cl bottle French beer

1 teaspoon dried parsley or rosemary

5 cm (2 in) garlic purée

1 vegetable stock cube or 1 rounded teaspoon chicken stock powder

50 g (2 oz) butter

1 heaped teaspoon cornflour

Mix the beer, parsley (or rosemary) and garlic purée. Marinade chicken in this mixture for at least 1 hour and up to 4 hours. Melt the butter in the frying pan, remove chicken from the marinade and fry in butter until lightly browned all over. Add marinade and crumble the stock cube into the mixture. Cook for 7 minutes, basting chicken with juices. Lift out chicken portions on to plates, blend the cornflour with a little water and add to the frying pan. Stir constantly until thickened. Season to taste and serve with rice, couscous or pasta.

Agneau Dijonais

2 lamb leg steaks
25cl bottle French beer
2 teaspoons Dijon mustard
5 cm (2 in) garlic purée
50 g (2 oz) creamed coconut
1 vegetable stock cube
2 tablespoons olive oil

Mix beer, mustard and garlic. Marinate the lamb in this mixture for 1-4 hours. Remove the lamb steaks from the marinade and fry in olive oil until lightly browned on both sides. Add marinade and crumble in the stock cube; then add the creamed coconut to the mixture. Cook for 8-10 minutes, turning once. Remove the lamb and place on plates. Return the stock and coconut to the heat and mix together and season to taste. Pour over the lamb. Serve with noodles or vegetable rice.

Ham Florentine

275 g (11 oz) packet frozen spinach
4 slices ham
50 g (2 oz) cheese, grated
2 heaped teaspoons dried milk
mustard

Cook the spinach according to the instructions on the packet, then spread on the bottom of a medium frying pan. Spread mustard on the ham and roll up. Place on top of spinach. Mix cheese and dried milk with five tablespoons of water. Coat ham with mix and place under a grill until golden brown. Serve with potatoes.

Main Meal Tortilla

4 size 3 eggs
100 g (4 oz) cooked meat or fish
100 g (4 oz) cooked/tinned vegetables
2 tablespoons oil
2 tablespoons water
Seasoning

Beat the eggs, add the water and seasoning and mix thoroughly. Heat the oil in a large frying pan, add meat/fish and vegetables. Heat through gently. Add the beaten egg mixture and continue to cook without stirring. When the omelette is set on the base and starting to brown, turn off the heat and place the frying pan under the grill; then allow to cook until completely set. Serve with salad, or on cold days with hot vegetables of your choice.

Combinations: ham and pineapple
salmon and asparagus
corned beef and peas
salmon and fresh tomato
tuna and sweetcorn
minced beef and spring onion
roast beef and carrots
chicken and sweetcorn

Orange and Apricot Pork

2 boneless loin pork chops

2 teaspoons cornflour

250ml carton orange and apricot drink

salt and pepper

1 teaspoon dried parsley

Heat the orange and apricot drink with the dried parsley. Put in the pork chops, basting with the juice. Cover and simmer for 15 minutes, turning the pork chops halfway through; add more liquid at this stage if necessary. Remove the pork. Thicken the juices left in the pan with cornflour blended with a little water. Add seasoning to taste.

Serve with boiled potatoes and carrots; garnish with orange slices.

Pork and Cauliflower

100 g (4 oz) lean pork

1 small cauliflower

1 tablespoon soy sauce

1 teaspoon sugar

1 vegetable stock cube

1 teaspoon instant mushroom soup

Cut the cauliflower into sprigs. Slice the pork and mix with soy sauce, sugar and soup powder. Heat the oil and stir fry the cauliflower for 1-2 minutes, sprinkling with the crumbled stock cube. Add a little water and cook until it bubbles. Put to one side. Wash the pan, heat more oil and fry the pork for about 12 minutes. Return the cauliflower to the pan and mix gently. Serve immediately with plain boiled rice.

Pork Provençale

I've been making this recipe both at home and on holiday for so many years I can't remember how it came about.

200 g (8 oz) diced pork
1 tablespoon olive oil
397g can peeled plum tomatoes
garlic salt
2 teaspoons Herbes de Provence

Fry the diced pork in olive oil, then season with garlic salt. Add the canned tomatoes, breaking into small pieces. Add the herbs and cook gently for 15 minutes. Serve with vegetables and a side salad.

Whiskey Pork

This is based on a recipe given to me by the chef in a wonderful restaurant in Donaghadee in Northern Ireland; hence the spelling of whiskey – although it tastes quite acceptable if Scotch is substituted for whiskey.

150 g (6 oz) fillet of pork
1 small chopped onion
1 clove garlic or 1 inch garlic purée
295 g can condensed mushroom soup
1 tablespoon Whiskey
1 teaspoon oil

Cut the fillet into strips. Fry the pork and onions together. Add crushed garlic (or garlic purée). Add the soup, without any extra water and whiskey. Heat through gently and adjust seasoning. Serve with rice.

Shepherd's Patties

100 g (4 oz) minced lamb

1 packet (4-6 servings) instant mashed potato

1 small onion (chopped)

1 teaspoon mint sauce

Dry fry the lamb and chopped onions for 7 - 10 minutes. Make up the instant mashed potato according to the instructions on the packet and mix in the mint sauce. Drain the lamb and onion, leaving fat behind in pan. Mix the made-up potato, lamb and onion, then shape into patties; fry in the pan with the leftover lamb fat until golden brown. Serve with mushy peas.

Boston Chilli

425 g can baked beans

¼ teaspoon chilli powder

205 g can minced beef

1 mug easy cook rice

Cook the rice in salted, boiling water. Meanwhile mix the baked beans and minced meat, adding chilli powder to taste. Heat gently. Drain rice. Serve the chilli mixture in the middle of the boiled rice.

Variation: omit the boiled rice, and serve with chunks of baguette to dip in.

Cottage Flan

205 g can minced beef and onion
1 savoury flan case
1 packet (4-6 servings) instant mashed potato

Warm the minced beef, then strain, reserving the gravy. Make up the instant mashed potato according to the instructions on the packet. Put the pastry case in the grill pan without wire rack. Warm through gently under the grill. Spoon in the beef, then cover with instant mashed potato. Put the flan back under the grill until the potato is browned. Serve with gravy reserved from the meat.

Three Pepper Burgers

Burgers coated in different peppers are a speciality of Northern Ireland and very easy to make yourself.

400 g frozen burgers (any variety, defrosted)
1 teaspoon paprika
⅛ teaspoon chilli or cayenne pepper.
1 teaspoon coarse ground black pepper.

Mix the peppers in a bowl. Take the burgers one at a time, put into the pepper mix and coat well, pressing the pepper mixture into each burger. Cook on a barbecue or under a grill. Serve with salad.

Marinade for Barbecue

1 tablespoon red wine
3 drops garlic oil
1 tablespoon olive oil
2 drops bay leaf oil
1 tablespoon lemon juice
salt and pepper

Mix all the ingredients together. Pour over the meat or fish to be barbecued and marinade for twenty four hours before cooking over hot barbecue coals.

Marinade on the move: put all the ingredients in a plastic bag and seal securely, using a self seal bag, wire closures, or knot or twist a plain bag and secure with a spring clothes peg.

Harvest sausage casserole

200 g (8 oz) pork chipolatas

Bramley apple (peeled & sliced)

300 g can sliced carrots

2 teaspoons dried onions

1 chicken or vegetable stock cube

3 slices bread

75 g (3 oz) grated cheese.

Soak the dried onions and dissolve the stock cube in 250mls boiling water. Fry the chipolata sausages until browned. Add the apple and fry until soft. Add the onion and stock mixture. Reduce the heat and simmer gently for 7 minutes. Drain the vegetables, add to the frying pan and stir gently. Remove from the heat. Place the slices of bread on top, pressing down gently to absorb some of the gravy. Sprinkle with grated cheese then put the frying pan under a preheated grill for 3-4 minutes. Serve with potatoes.

Shih-Chin Stir Fry

This recipe is of Chinese origin, adapted for life on the open road.

    50 g (2 oz) cooked chicken meat
    50 g (2 oz) boiled ham
    25 g (1 oz) peeled prawns
    50 g (2 oz) mushrooms (button or sliced if larger)
    ⅛ diced cucumber
    2 size 3 eggs, beaten
    4 chopped spring onions
    Handful fresh or frozen peas
    1 tablespoon sherry

Stir fry the chicken, ham, prawns, peas, cucumber and mushrooms for about 1 minute. Add the sherry and then put to one side. Heat some oil and make an omelette with the eggs, but break it up before it is fully cooked. Return all the other ingredients to the pan and cook together for a few seconds. Serve with chopped spring onions sprinkled on top.

Apple and Coriander Chicken

2 boneless, skinless chicken breasts
1 teaspoon cornflour
Garlic salt
250mls (½pint) pure apple juice
Salt and pepper
1 level teaspoon ground coriander
6 dessertspoons double cream

Heat the apple juice in pan, add coriander and garlic salt. Place the chicken portions in a frying pan, baste with juice, then cover the pan and cook over gentle heat for 15-20 minutes, turning the chicken breasts halfway through. Lift out the chicken. Blend the cornflour with a little water, then add to the juices left in the frying pan; heat to thicken. Add cream and stir over gentle heat. DO NOT BOIL! Add salt and pepper to taste. Pour this sauce over the chicken. Serve with plain boiled rice and a side salad.

Barbecue Chicken

2 fillets chicken breast (with or without sk in)
1 tablespoon tomato ketchup.
2 tablespoons sherry
2 teaspoons sugar

Mix the ketchup, sherry and sugar. Marinade the chicken for at least 2 hours, (put in plastic bag to take up less room). Take the wire rack out of the grill pan. Put chicken in the grill pan and grill for 15 minutes, turning frequently. (This could be a little smoky so try to leave the door open if possible). Serve with lemon wedges. Alternatively, grill on an open barbecue where you won't have to worry about filling the caravan full of cooking smoke.

Chicken Fricassee

150 g (6 oz) chicken fillet chopped
1 heaped dessertspoon dried onion
1 rasher middle cut bacon chopped
1 chicken stock cube
4 tablespoons dry white wine
50 g (2 oz) mushrooms (sliced)
35 g (1½ oz) dried milk

Make up the stock and add the dried onions to soak. Fry the chicken and bacon lightly until sealed. Add the stock with onions and wine. Simmer for 10 minutes, add the mushrooms, simmer for further 10 minutes. Use some of the cooking juice to blend the dried milk then add to the pan; reheat, but do not boil. Serve with rice and side salad.

Golden Chicken

220mls (⅓ pint) milk
2 cooked chicken portions, removed from the bone.
10 g sachet instant golden vegetable soup
100 g (4 oz) button mushrooms
1 red pepper, de-seeded & cut into strips
Oil for frying

Fry the mushrooms and pepper until tender. Stir in the soup powder, adding the milk gradually. Cook over a gentle heat, stirring constantly until thickened. Add the chicken and stir gently until heated through. Serve with vegetables or over toast.

Spicy Peanut Chicken

2 boneless chicken breasts
1 tablespoon smooth peanut butter
1 pinch cayenne or chilli pepper
2 tablespoons wine, sherry or port

Mix together the peanut butter, wine and pepper until smooth, coat the chicken with the mixture and leave to marinade for at least one hour. Heat a little oil in a frying pan. Cook the chicken and mixture for fifteen minutes, basting frequently, taking care not to burn the chicken. Add more liquid (water or wine) half way through, then reduce to thicken again. Serve with rice or vegetables.

Strawberry Chicken

I visited an International Food Fair in Belfast, tasted a dish called strawberry chicken and was so enchanted I just had to recreate it myself.

2 boneless, skinless chicken breasts
250ml (½pint) carton strawberry drink
garlic salt or onion
salt and pepper
cornflour
6 dessertspoons double cream
a few fresh strawberries if available

Heat the drink with the garlic salt. Put in the chicken, baste with juice. Cover and simmer for 15 minutes, turning the chicken over halfway through. Remove the chicken. Thicken the liquid with blended cornflour. Add the cream, then reheat (DO NOT BOIL!). Add seasoning to taste. Pour the sauce over the chicken. Serve with plain boiled rice and a side salad.

Turkey Carolans

This is another recipe with Irish connections. I had the good fortune to spend a year in and around Belfast, which introduced me to many new ingredients and styles of cooking.

100 g (4 oz) cooked turkey breast

100mls (4fl oz) Carolans Irish cream liqueur

100mls (4fl oz) double cream

2 tablespoon dried onions

100 g (4 oz) mushrooms (sliced)

2 drops of garlic oil

1 tablespoon olive oil

Soak onions in enough boiling water to cover. Fry the mushrooms in olive oil with garlic oil added. Drain the onions and add. Fry gently, as it will spit if cooked over a high heat. Cut the cooked turkey breast into strips and add to pan. Heat through. Add the Carolans and the cream. Heat very gently taking care not to boil. Season to taste. Serve with plain boiled rice or pasta and a side salad.

Cranberry Minted Turkey

2 turkey breast fillets
250ml cranberry juice drink
2 teaspoons mint sauce
4 heaped tablespoons dried milk
50 g (2 oz) butter
1 heaped teaspoon cornflour

Fry the turkey fillets in butter until lightly browned. Add cranberry juice and mint sauce. Simmer for 10-15 minutes, turning once at the halfway point. Remove the turkey from juice. Take the pan off the heat and sprinkle in the dried milk. Return to the heat and stir constantly until smooth. Blend the cornflour with a little water, then add to the pan, stirring constantly. Add seasoning to taste. Pour the sauce over the turkey. Serve with an accompaniment of your choice.

Sweet and Sour Chicken

200 g (8 oz) diced chicken
2 heaped teaspoons cornflour
175 g (6 oz) medium onion, sliced
4 teaspoons sugar
2 tablespoons tomato ketchup
1 teaspoon vinegar
225 g can pineapple chunks
1 tablespoon sunflower oil

Heat the oil in large frying pan. Add the meat and fry until lightly browned. Add the sliced onions and cook until transparent. Turn down the heat and add the pineapple chunks, reserving the juice. Combine pineapple juice, tomato ketchup, sugar, vinegar and cornflour, and mix until smooth. Add to the meat and onion mix and stir quickly until sauce has thickened and coated the meat pieces. Water can be added if required. Serve with plain boiled rice.

Stir Fry Curry with Mango

150 g (6 oz) pork, beef fillet or chicken, sliced
1 mango (sliced)
1 small onion (chopped)
4 teaspoons curry powder (mild)
2 teaspoons desiccated coconut
1 chicken or beef stock cube as appropriate
1 tablespoon vegetable oil
375mls (½ pint) water

In a large frying pan, heat the oil. Add the meat and stir quickly to seal. Reduce the heat and add the onion. Fry for 7 - 10 minutes. Remove from the heat, add water, coconut and curry powder. Stir. Crumble in the stock cube and stir again. Continue cooking for another 7 minutes. Add the mango, stir and heat through gently. Serve immediately with rice, pasta, couscous or new potatoes.

Chicken Paysanne

4 chicken fillet portions
4 fresh tomatoes, chopped
1 tablespoon French mustard
75 g (3 oz) butter
1 teaspoon Herbes de Provence
2 tablespoons tomato ketchup
salt and pepper

Spread the French mustard on the chicken fillets. Melt the butter in large frying pan. Cook the chicken fillets for 6 minutes on each side; then add the tomatoes, ketchup and herbs. Add seasoning to taste, then cook for a further 2-3 minutes. Serve with rice or creamed potatoes.

Drover's Patties

100 g (4 oz) minced beef
1 small onion, chopped
1 packet (4-6 servings) instant mashed potato
1 teaspoon mustard or horseradish sauce

Dry fry the beef and onion for 7-10 minutes. Make up the instant mashed potato according to the instructions on the packet, then mix in the mustard or horseradish sauce. Drain the onion and beef mixture, leaving the fat behind in the pan. Mix the spiced potato with the beef and onion, shape into patties, then fry them in pan with leftover beef fat, adding a little oil if necessary. Serve with Mushy Peas.

Ploughman's Patties

100 g (4 oz) Cheddar cheese
1 small onion
1 packet (4-6 servings) instant mashed potato
1 teaspoon dried parsley
oil for frying

Fry the onions until soft in a small amount of oil. Mix the dried parsley with the instant mashed potato powder/flakes then make up the instant mashed potato according to the instructions on the packet. Drain the onions and add to the potato, leaving the oil in the pan. Grate the cheese and add this to the mashed potato mixture; then shape into patties then fry in the left over oil. Serve with mushy peas.

Corned Beef and Beetroot Hash

200 g (8 oz) corned beef

150 g (6 oz) cooked beetroot (not pickled), chopped

6 canned new potatoes, chopped

2 tablespoons butter

1 tablespoon dried onion

Salt & pepper

Reconstitute the onion; drain well. Melt the butter in a frying pan and fry the onion gently until transparent. Add the beetroot and potato. Break up the corned beef and add to the vegetables with the salt and pepper; mix well. Cook over low heat until lightly browned on the bottom.

Serve with salad.

Mild Pan-Fried Liver

200 g (8 oz) pigs liver (cut small)

150ml (⅓ pint) milk

salt and pepper

cornflour or flour

oil for frying

Soak the liver in milk for 24 hours. Drain and discard the blood and milk mixture (or give it to the dog if you have one!). Mix the flour with salt and pepper. Dredge each liver piece in the flour mixture and fry in hot oil until golden.

Fish and Seafood

Fried Cod and Cucumber

2 portions cod fillet (fresh or frozen, defrosted)
½ cucumber
50 g (2 oz) butter or margarine
lemon juice
salt & pepper

Season the cod portions with salt and pepper. Heat the butter or margarine and fry the cod on one side for 5 minutes. Peel the cucumber and cut into strips. Turn the cod portions over and add the cucumber and a sprinkle of lemon juice. Cook for further 5 minutes. Serve with vegetables of your choice.

Variation: Add strips of cooked ham with cucumber.

Lomi Lomi (A Hawaiian Dish)

240 g can red salmon
1 bunch spring onions, chopped
3 fresh tomatoes, diced
salt

Remove the skin and bones from the canned salmon and drain excess liquid. Flake the salmon coarsely with a fork and combine with the other ingredients. Serve well chilled, with toast or salad.

Lemon Minted Cod

We'd had a wonderful day, riding up and down the preserved railway at Severn Valley. Steam traction in all its forms is one of my delights, and now we strolled back towards the motorcaravan. We'd parked in a beautiful spot, just at the end of the road at Arley, right on the banks of the River Severn; not all the best spots are on campsites. On the way past the pub we collected two bottles of Sam Smith's Old Pale Ale, which we intended to drink with our evening meal. The meal was supposed to be fresh cod and parsley sauce, but cooking is not always predictable and accidents happen. Some of the most famous recipes were created by accident. It happened that I was gently frying the cod when I remembered that I had a bottle of lemon juice on board.

"That'll add a bit of piquancy," I thought, "it'll offset the flat taste of the ready-made parsley sauce."

What I had forgotten, however, was that the lemon juice had long ago lost its sprinkler top. Off came the screw cap, over went the lemon juice. Nearly all of it – about half a bottle. Instead of being a light sprinkle, the cod was now swimming again, only in lemon juice, not sea water. It was too late to drain it off, and now the fish would be unbearably tart. It needed sweetening and seasoning, possibly herbs, I thought. Looking through the cupboard I came across a jar of mint sauce – ingredients sugar, vinegar, mint. Perfect. I added a spoonful to the lemon juice and then poached the cod in it. It tasted wonderful and much better than the originally planned meal.

The next morning, there was another surprise for us. We awoke to find the van rocking alarmingly from side to side. Concerned, we rushed to the window. Surrounding us on all sides was a herd of cows! Someone had left a gate open, and the cows, curious about our red van, had come to investigate. Once they arrived, they'd decided it was a pretty good object to have a scratch upon, and now we were completely cut off by the cows pushing and milling around, each one anxious to try the strange scratching post. We had to wait for a farmer to come and chase them back into the field. I'm fairly certain, from the look he gave us, that he blamed us for the incident, but we were totally innocent. The next time we visited the Severn Valley Railway, we stopped on a camp site!

4 cod steaks (fresh or frozen, defrosted)

2 tablespoons lemon juice

2 teaspoons mint sauce

2 tablespoons sunflower oil

Heat the sunflower oil in a frying pan, then fry the cod portions gently for 3 minutes on each side. Combine the lemon juice and mint then add the mixture to the pan. Simmer gently for 4-5 minutes, basting the cod with juices. Serve with the accompaniment of your choice.

Creamed Sweetcorn and Prawns

200 g can prawns

½ 245 g can creamed sweetcorn

1 vegetable stock cube

½ cup water

Drain the canned prawns reserving the liquid. Heat the prawn juice and water in saucepan, then crumble in the stock cube and stir until dissolved. Add the half can of creamed sweetcorn. Adjust the seasoning to taste. Add the prawns, then heat gently but thoroughly. Serve poured over vegetable rice.

Mackerel Pie

125 g can mackerel in tomato sauce
1 sachet instant mushroom soup
1 packet (4-6 servings) instant mashed potato
Herbes de Provence

Place the mackerel in a small frying pan, then break up with a fork. Add the herbs and mix well. Add the sachet of soup mix to the dry instant mashed potato powder and mix well together. Make up the instant mashed potato according to the instructions on the packet. Pile the potato mixture on top of the mackerel. Heat gently for 7 minutes, then transfer the pan to the grill and heat the top until the potato mix starts to brown.

Pan Fried Trout

2 whole trout,
fresh, cleaned or
frozen, defrosted.
cornflour or flour
salt and pepper
olive oil

Sprinkle the trout lightly with salt and pepper inside and out. Coat well with flour. Heat the oil in a frying pan. Fry the trout over a medium heat until crisp and brown on both sides (5-10 minutes per side). Serve immediately.

Plaice & Crab Parcels

2 white plaice fillets

43g can dressed crab

2 large cabbage leaves

For the sauce:

397g can plum tomatoes drained

100 g (4 oz) fresh mushrooms sliced or 1 small can button mushrooms, drained

1 heaped teaspoon dried parsley

50 g (2 oz) butter

few drops lemon juice or $\frac{1}{4}$ of a lemon.

Lay down the fish fillets and make several incisions on the flesh side. Spread the fillets with the dressed crab and roll up. Place in a cabbage leaf and wrap. Then wrap each parcel tightly in cling film and place into boiling water for 5 minutes. Remove cling film and place on a dish.

For the sauce: Chop the tomatoes then heat the butter in a frying pan. If using fresh mushrooms fry them gently for two minutes, then add the tomatoes. Or, if using canned mushrooms, add together with tomatoes and fry for one minute. Add a squeeze of lemon or a few drops of juice. Serve the fish with new potatoes boiled in skins. Spoon the sauce over both fish and potatoes.

Salmon Dickies

I used to call this recipe Salmon Duchesse, but my husband, who is a chef, suggested that this term was not quite correct. My word processor didn't have Duchesse in the dictionary, and suggested Dickies as an alternative; we liked the name so much it stuck.

1 packet (4-6 servings) instant mashed potato

50 g (2 oz) parsley butter

213g can salmon

2 tablespoons sunflower oil

N.B. The parsley butter must be as cold as possible. If fridge is available then leave it in the fridge until required.

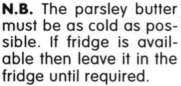

Take the wire rack out of the grill pan and lightly oil the base. Make up the instant mashed potato with slightly less water than stated on the packet (to make a stiffer mix). Open the can of salmon and drain off the liquid. When the potato has cooled use a third of it to shape into 4 round patties and place in the grill pan. Make a small depression in the centre. Divide the salmon into 4 and place on top of the patties. Add a small pat of parsley butter on top of the salmon. Spoon or pipe remaining potato on top until salmon and butter is covered. If a spoon is used, leave potato surface rough with small peaks. Brush, or preferably spray the top lightly with oil. Preheat the grill then place grill pan under and turn down the heat to low. After 5 minutes turn the heat up to brown the surface. Serve with vegetables of your choice; using any remaining parsley butter on the vegetables.

Spanish Cod

Without the usual accompaniment of Spanish Tummy!

125mls (¼ pint) orange juice

2 tablespoons dried peppers

2 portions cod fillet (fresh or frozen, defrosted)

1 tablespoon tomato ketchup

Add the orange juice to the dried peppers and simmer for five minutes. Fry the cod portions in a little oil until they are barely cooked. Add the tomato ketchup to the pepper and juice mixture and then mix thoroughly. Slide the cod fillets into the pepper sauce and cook for eight minutes. Remove the cod fillets onto hot plates. Reduce the sauce by further cooking if necessary, then pour it over the cod. Serve with rice and/or salad.

Prawn Gumbo

213g can prawns

400 g can tomatoes

295 g can cream of tomato soup

425 g can mixed vegetables

1 small can new potatoes (not minted)

1 heaped tablespoon sliced, canned peaches

1 level tablespoon sultanas

½ teaspoon cayenne pepper (or less, according to taste)

3 teaspoons cornflour

2-5 cm (1-2 in) garlic purée, according to taste

1 vegetable or chicken stock cube

salt and pepper to taste

Mix the cornflour with some of the tomato soup until blended.

Put it in a large saucepan with the rest of the soup, the can of tomatoes, garlic purée and cayenne pepper. Stir over a gentle heat until thickened, then crumble the stock cube into the mixture. Drain the vegetables and cut up the potatoes, then add these to the saucepan. Add the other ingredients and reheat gently. Serve with rice or couscous.

Sauces

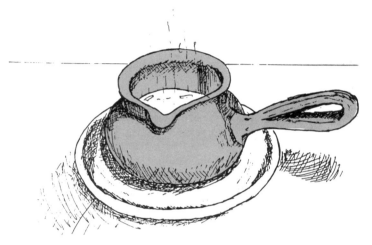

Creamed Cauliflower Sauce

1 medium cauliflower or small packet, frozen
2 teaspoons cornflour
1 vegetable stock cube
25 g (1 oz) butter or margarine
150mls (6floz) milk

Cook the cauliflower florets until soft. Drain and mash. Add the milk, crumbled vegetable cube and cornflower. Heat the mixture gently until the sauce thickens. Serve with pasta, or as an accompaniment to meat or fish.

Variation: use single cream instead of milk for a really creamy taste.

Waldorf sauce

1 packet instant white sauce

coarsely chopped walnut pieces

1 dessertspoons sultanas

½ dessert apple, cored, peeled and chopped

Make up the sauce then add the other ingredients. Serve over vegetables.

Variation: if you use a ready-made sauce, it can be used cold as a salad accompaniment.

Marie Rose Sauce

3 tablespoons salad cream

1 tablespoon tomato ketchup

Mix the ingredients until thoroughly combined. Use over seafood such as prawns, crab or crabsticks.

Chilli Sauce

2 tablespoons tomato ketchup

1 teaspoon lemon juice

¼ teaspoon chilli or cayenne pepper

Salt and pepper to taste

Mix the ingredients until thoroughly combined. Chill well and serve as a dip or with cold meats.

Cucumber Raita

¼ cucumber, diced
125ml natural yoghurt
½ teaspoon mint sauce
salt

Sprinkle the diced cucumber with salt, leave for half an hour, then rinse and drain. Pour the natural yoghurt over the cucumber. Add the mint sauce then mix well. Serve with salads or cold and hot meats. It is especially good with curries.

Desserts

Strawberry Shortcake

1 packet trifle sponges or plain, stale cake
1 can strawberries
1 teaspoon desiccated coconut

Place the trifle sponges or plain stale cake in the bottom of a dish; spoon the strawberries and juice over the top. Sprinkle the desiccated coconut over the top of the strawberries then chill well. Serve with aerosol cream or vanilla ice cream.

Fried Bananas

2 firm bananas
½ teaspoon cinnamon
1 dessertspoon lemon juice
1 tablespoon sugar
50 g (2 oz) butter

Peel the bananas and cut in half lengthwise. Sprinkle with lemon juice. Heat the butter in a frying pan and fry bananas until browned on both sides. Sprinkle them with cinnamon and sugar.

Serve with Greek yoghurt.

Variation: heat marmalade and 1 tablespoon of Rum instead of cinnamon and sugar.

Chocolate Mandarin Fool

1 packet Chocolate instant custard
2 mandarin orange yoghurts
500mls (1pt) Orange Juice
1 chocolate flake

Heat the orange juice and use in place of water to make up the custard. Allow to cool, stirring occasionally to prevent skinning. Stir in one yoghurt. Spoon into glasses or bowls. Top with the remaining yoghurt. Crumble the Flake and sprinkle on top.

Chocolate Crunch Pears

2 ready-made chocolate puddings
411g can pear slices
3 digestive biscuits

Crumble the digestive biscuits. Add two-thirds of the biscuit crumble to one chocolate pudding and mix. Put this mixture in the bottom of two glass bowls. Drain the pear slices and arrange on top of mixture. Coat the pears with the remaining chocolate pudding, then sprinkle with the remaining digestive biscuit crumble. Serve within 1 hour.

Chocolate Orange Swirl

1 packet instant custard
300 g small can mandarin orange segments
1 chocolate Flake

Make up the custard according to the instructions on the packet, using the juice from the mandarin oranges as part of the liquid. Divide into two. Crumble the Flake into one half, mixing until melted. Reserve some orange segments for decoration, then break up the remainder and add to the other part of the custard, then mix thoroughly. Put equal amounts of each type of custard into glasses/bowls and swirl together, but do not over-mix. Decorate with reserved oranges. Serve when cold.

Fruited Ambrosia

300 g can mandarin segments
2 maraschino cherries, halved
25 g (1 oz) desiccated coconut

Put a third of the oranges in a dish, then sprinkle with a third of the coconut. Repeat twice more. Decorate with cherries. Chill for at least one hour, but will keep overnight. Serve with hot or cold rice pudding.

Hot Chocolate Crunch Pears

1 packet instant chocolate custard
411 g can pear slices
3 digestive biscuits

Drain the pears, reserving the liquid. Add water to pear liquid to make up to the amount stated on custard packet. Make up custard, using the pear/water mixture. Crumble the digestive biscuits. Arrange the pear slices in two glass dishes. Coat the pears with the chocolate custard then sprinkle thickly with digestive biscuits. Serve immediately, while still hot.

Jewelled Semolina

1 packet instant semolina.
A few pieces Turkish delight (preferably mixed colours).

Cut up the Turkish delight into small dice. Make up the semolina according to the instructions on the packet. Stir in the Turkish delight then pour into glasses or bowls to set. Serve cold.

Variation: Pooh Bear Semolina: replace Turkish delight with broken honeycomb bar.

Madeira trifle

2 slices madeira cake
2 bananas
4 tablespoon sherry
carton or can of ready-made custard or aerosol cream

Break the cake into pieces, placing in two large glasses or fruit bowls. Put 2 tablespoons of sherry over each serving. Slice the bananas, placing them on top of the cake. Cover with ready-made custard or aerosol cream. Serve. Note: if using cream, serve immediately.

Strawberry Delight

If you use the sugar-free Delight Instant Pudding, you get the taste of luxury cheesecake for about a third of the calories.

1 packet strawberry Delight Instant Pudding (sugar free or ordinary)
1 small punnet strawberries
4 digestive biscuits
1 large or 4 small cartons of natural yoghurt

Crush each biscuit and put in bottom of individual glasses or a large flat-bottomed bowl. Mash the strawberries, reserving some for decoration. Mix the yoghurt and mashed strawberries together. Add the Delight powder and mix QUICKLY; it will go very stiff. Put the mixture in the glasses or bowl on top of the crushed biscuit. Decorate with reserved strawberries. Serve.
N.B. Eat the same day as it will not keep longer.
Variations: Canned mandarin oranges and Orange Delight
Bananas and Butterscotch Delight.
Peach Delight and almonds (flaked).
Raspberry Delight and canned or fresh raspberries.
Lemon Delight and raisin (soak raisins first)
Muesli instead of digestive biscuits.

Tipsy Pudding

225 g can pineapple chunks
425 g carton custard
stale cake
glacé cherries to decorate
3 tablespoon sherry

Break up the cake roughly and soak with sherry. (Do this in a plastic bag if you are on the move). Drain the pineapple and put chunks in bottom of glasses or bowls. Cover with the sherried cake, then a layer of custard. Place a glacé cherry in middle to decorate.

Melon and Ginger Cocktail

This also makes a refreshing starter for a meal.
Pieces of water melon
Pieces of honeydew or other sweet melon
1 level teaspoon ground ginger
1 carton natural yoghurt
brown sugar

Cut up the melon. Mix the ginger and yoghurt and use this to coat the melon. Place in glasses and sprinkle with brown sugar.

Fruit Compote

1 medium eating apple
411g can mango slices
225 g can pineapple chunks
25 g (1 oz) sultanas
2 tablespoons Cointreau
1 tablespoon sugar

Peel and core the apple. Slice thinly. Drain the mangoes and pineapple, reserving the juice and mix the fruits together. Put the sultanas in the juice to soak. Put the sliced apples in a saucepan with 3 tablespoons of fruit juice and the sugar. Heat, stirring constantly until the apple is soft. Cut up the mango into chunks. Add the pineapple, juice, sultanas and mango to the saucepan. Heat for a further 5 minutes. Add the Cointreau to the compote and refrigerate.

Kiwi Jelly Salad

2 kiwi fruit
1 tub custard
1 packet lime jelly

Make up the jelly with half the usual amount of water. Chill until set firm. Cut into cubes. Peel and roughly chop the Kiwi fruit, then put them in bottom of a bowl. Cover with a layer of custard, then the jelly cubes.
Variations: canned mandarins & orange jelly.
bananas (sliced) & peach jelly.

Black Forest Meringues

2 meringue nests
1 chocolate flake
2 slices chocolate swiss roll
1 black cherry yoghurt

Place a slice of swiss roll in each meringue nest. Cover with yoghurt and sprinkle with crumbled chocolate flake.

Coffee mandarin syllabub

1 dessertspoon instant coffee (not freeze-dried)
1 mandarin yoghurt
125ml carton whipping cream
1 tablespoon white wine

Beat the cream and coffee powder/granules together until stiff. Mix in the white wine and yoghurt. Spoon into glasses or bowls to serve.

Black Cherry Fruit Crescent

1 can cherry pie filling
500ml tub natural Greek yoghurt

Reserve 2 tablespoons of juice from the pie filling. In 4 bowls, arrange the pie filling in a crescent along one side. Place the yoghurt alongside each crescent of fruit to fill the bowl. Drizzle the reserved juice over the yoghurt, then using a cocktail stick, pull it through the yoghurt to make swirls.

Apple Oat Crunch

8 Oat crunch biscuits
400 g can apple pie filling
425 g carton custard

Place the biscuits in plastic bag and crush. In 4 large wine glasses or small bowls place a layer of crushed biscuits then place a layer of apple; repeat until 2 cm (¾") is left in the glass. Finish off with a layer of custard. Garnish with half a Maraschino cherry or a small piece of flake chocolate.

Variation: instead of custard, just before serving pile high with aerosol cream.

Snacks

French Bread Pizza

French bread, fresh or stale
100 g (4 oz) grated cheese (Cheddar or mozzarella)
2 economy burgers
1 tomato
cayenne pepper
1 tablespoon ketchup

Allow the burgers to defrost then break them up with a fork. Fry without oil but with seasonings until cooked and granular. Mix in the ketchup and chopped fresh tomato. Slice a third from the baguette, then cut the piece in half lengthways. Spread the cut baguette with the mixture, then cover with grated cheese. Put each piece in a grill pan with the wire rack removed and grill until cheese starts to bubble.

Garlic Bread

French bread
crushed garlic or garlic purée
butter or margarine
parsley

Mix together the butter, garlic and parsley to taste, then spread it on slices of baguette. Place the bread butter side up in the grill pan and grill until the edges of the bread start to toast. Sprinkle with salt and pepper. Use an accompaniment to Italian food or salads.

Club Sandwiches

6 slices bread
butter
2 slices chicken or turkey breast
2 slices boiled ham
shredded lettuce
sliced tomato

Toast the bread and spread all the slices with butter. On two of the buttered slices lay chicken and ham. Place another slice of toast butter side down on top of chicken and ham. Place sliced tomato and lettuce on top and finish with last slice of toast. Hold together with cocktail sticks in each corner. Cut diagonally into quarters. Serve with Marie Rose sauce (page 66).

Vegetable 'Samosas'

4 slices wholemeal bread
2 size 3 eggs
425 g can mixed vegetables
3 teaspoons mild curry powder

Cut the crusts from the slices of bread. Drain the vegetables and mix with the curry powder. Then spread the curried vegetables evenly on two slices of bread, cover to make sandwiches and press lightly. Beat the eggs well and coat each sandwich; allow the bread to soak up some of the egg. Fry the sandwich in a small amount of oil until golden brown. Cut into triangles and serve hot or cold with salad.

Pork Sausage and Apple Rolls

200 g (8 oz) pork sausages

50 g (2 oz) luncheon roll

2 heaped teaspoons apple sauce

Cook the sausages and allow to cool. Using one piece of luncheon meat for each sausage coat a slice with apple sauce. Wrap a piece around each sausage, sauce side in, and secure with a cocktail stick. Place in a grill pan with wire rack removed and heat gently. Discard cocktail sticks before serving. May be eaten hot or cold.

Chicken and Blue Stilton Toasts

213g can chicken

150 g (5 oz) Blue Stilton cheese

25 g (1 oz) butter or margarine

2 cm (1 in) garlic purée (tube)

4 slices bread brown or white

salt and pepper

Cream together the butter or margarine and garlic purée. Toast the bread on one side. Spread the untoasted side with the butter and garlic mixture. Slice the chicken and arrange on top. Season to taste. Slice the Stilton and cover the chicken. Place under a hot grill until the cheese is melted. Serve garnished with sliced fresh tomato.

Blue Cheese Balls

125 g (4 oz) blue cheese
72g (2 oz) chopped walnuts
1 packet (4-6 servings) instant mashed potato

Make up the instant mashed potato according to the instructions on the packet. Mix in the chopped walnuts. Cut the cheese into 1 cm (½ ins) cubes. Coat each cube with the potato/walnut mixture. Shallow fry, turning gently until golden brown. Serve with salad.

Baked Eggs

4 size 3 eggs
75 g (3 oz) cheese, grated
100 g (4 oz) mushrooms, chopped
2 cups lettuce, shredded
1 teaspoon Worcester sauce
1 tablespoon oil for frying

Stir fry the lettuce and mushrooms in a large frying pan, and then mix in the Worcester sauce. Carefully break four eggs into the pan. Cook gently for 2-3 minutes, until the eggs are set on the bottom. Sprinkle with cheese, put the frying pan under the grill until the eggs are cooked and the cheese is melted. Serve with salad or vegetables of your choice.

Eggs Piggyback

300 g canned luncheon meat
Toast
1 per person size 3 eggs

Cut the luncheon meat in ½ cm (¼ in) slices. Fry until the surface is crispy. Fry, poach or scramble the eggs. Place the luncheon meat on the toast; top with egg. Serve with slices of fresh tomato. Makes a good breakfast.

Note: fried luncheon meat makes a cheap substitute for bacon in an English breakfast. Don't attempt to grill it – it sticks like glue to the grill pan rack.

Turkey Sausage and Cranberry Rolls

200 g (8 oz) turkey sausages
2 heaped teaspoon cranberry sauce
50 g (2 oz) chicken roll

Cook the sausages and allow to cool. Using 1 piece chicken roll for each sausage, spread it with cranberry sauce (if using cranberry jelly heat it to enable it to spread more evenly). Wrap a sauce covered chicken roll slice around each sausage, cranberry side inwards, then secure with a cocktail stick. Place in a grill pan with wire rack removed and heat gently. Discard the cocktail sticks before serving. Serve hot or cold.

Coddled Mushrooms

50 g (2 oz) sliced mushrooms
2 tablespoons ready-made white sauce
2 size 3 eggs
salt and pepper
a little oil or butter

Fry the mushrooms gently in oil or butter for 2 minutes. Divide equally into four, placing in cups from an egg poacher Beat the sauce and the eggs together, season and divide between cups. Poach gently until set. Serve on toast with slices of fresh tomato and watercress.

Sandwich Fillings

Tuna & Sweetcorn

213g can flaked tuna
canned sweetcorn
2 tablespoons mayonnaise

Drain tuna and sweetcorn and mix all ingredients.
Variation: use canned sweetcorn with peppers.
Use as filling in French bread, Pitta bread, rolls or sandwiches.

Shrimp & Egg

200 g can broken shrimps
2 size 3 eggs
50 g (2 oz) Cheddar cheese
1 tablespoon mayonnaise

Hard boil the eggs and allow to cool. Drain the shrimps; peel and chop the eggs. Combine all ingredients and use as a filling.

Tangy Beef

150 g (6 oz) cooked, sliced beef
1 tablespoon mayonnaise
1 heaped teaspoon horseradish sauce
8 slices of wholemeal bread

Mix the mayonnaise and horseradish. Spread on eight slices of bread. Put beef on four slices and make up sandwiches with the other four slices.
Variation: substitute mustard for horseradish.

Mediterranean Filling

50 g (2 oz) boiled ham
50 g (2 oz) lunch tongue
1 tablespoon tomato purée
½ teaspoon garlic salt

Cut the cooked meat into Juliennes (thin matchstick-length strips). Add the tomato purée and garlic salt then mix until the meat is evenly coated.
Variation: add 4 chopped olives.

Roast Pork and Apple

Apple sauce sometimes comes in rather large jars for use in caravans; you end up throwing much of it away. However, you can get apple purée in baby food ranges. The size of the jar is just right for one meal or for making up sandwiches.

150 g (6 oz) sliced pork
2 tablespoons apple sauce or purée

Spread the apple on all slices of bread then make up sandwiches with the cooked pork.

Chunky Cheese and Apple

150 g (6 oz) Cheddar cheese
2 desert apples

Slice the Cheddar, then core and slice apples. Assemble the sandwiches with a layer of cheese and a layer of apple.

Prawn Cocktail Filling

200 g can prawns
1 iceberg lettuce
Marie Rose sauce (page 66)

Shred the lettuce into a bowl. Add the prawns and sauce then mix until ingredients are evenly coated. This goes especially well on baguettes.

A Whirlwind Tour of The Regional Foods of Britain

London – famous for its jellied eels, of course, which you either love or loathe. These can be found on stalls in the East End, which also sell shellfish such as cockles, mussels and whelks. In Hackney, Ridleys is famous for its 24 hour bagel shop and pie and mash shops can still be found. Many cosmopolitan samples of food can be found in London.

Kent – the 'garden of England', home of hops, fruit and market gardens. Sadly, many regional specialities have disappeared in Kent, although you can look out for produce made with the abundant local cherries. There are also farmhouse ciders to be found and Kent has several established vineyards, usually announced by the brown tourist road signs.

Dorset – home of the famous Moore's Dorset Knob Biscuits. These are found at grocers and delicatessens throughout Dorset. Less well known, but worth trying out, are the local speciality found in fish and chips shops. These are pea fritters, which basically consist of a handful-sized ball of mushy peas, which are then dipped into batter and deep-fried.

Wiltshire – once known as 'the home of the pig', was famous for pork pies and sausages. With the closure of many factories, the purely local products are becoming very difficult to find, although you may strike lucky at a small butcher's who still makes his own products. Look out particularly for white pudding, which is made from oatmeal, pork fat and plenty of seasoning. Haslet – mixture of meat, breadcrumbs and herbs formed into a loaf and then cooked and sliced is excellent in sandwiches. Its smaller cousin, the faggot, is very tasty in a rich gravy and served with vegetables.

Somerset – this county seems to swim in farmhouse cider, much of it still made in a centuries-old fashion, and extremely palatable. Look out for the brown tourist signs announcing the presence of a farm which makes the cider and pay a visit. All that I've ever visited are more than happy to discuss the cider-making, and ply you with tasters of their product. Most also produce excellent cold-pressed apple juices, but watch out for the scrumpy – best not to touch a drop if you're driving! Incidentally, the word 'cider' comes from the Latin sicera, meaning strong drink. You have been warned! Bath, in East Somerset, is famous for Bath Olivers – a type of cracker which is excellent with cheese, Bath Buns and Sally Lunn Cakes – both of which are made from sweet, yeasted dough.

Devon – renowned, of course for its clotted cream and associated products – scones, toffee and fudge. Less well known, but very tasty is a seasonal sweet bread known as Saffron Cake. This is usually found in baker's shops at Easter, but is becoming less seasonal. Of course, it does taste good with clotted cream!

Cornwall – Cornish pasties are a much adulterated snack in most parts of the British Isles. However, if you search carefully, you may find real pasties in Cornwall. Pasties were the original 'lunch pack' – a neat package containing a complete meal. The pasties taken to work by the tin miners even contained savoury at one end and sweet at the other – two courses in one package. The fold of pastry at the top, or handle, was used to hold the pasty by so that a man who had a dirty job could use this to hold his pasty, and then throw that last, dirty, morsel away. Although pilchard fishing ended just before the first World War with the disappearance of the pilchards from Cornish shores, Stargazey Pie can still be found. This is a fish pie where the heads of pilchards poke through the pastry crust – gazing at the stars. Clotted cream is also abundant in Cornwall.

Wales – Bara Brith is common throughout Wales, indeed almost every baker's shop will sell this sweet bread. It is flavoured with currants, raisins, candied peel and mixed spice. It is a close relative of Barm Brack from Ireland, Bannocks from Scotland and Lardy cake from England. Faggots are to be found in Wales, but traditionally oatmeal replaces the breadcrumbs used in English faggots, and sometimes pieces of apple are included in the mixture. Laver is an edible seaweed (Porphyra umbilicalis) which grows on the western coast of Britain. This purplish-coloured seaweed is nowadays imported from Scotland to satisfy local demand. It is processed into a brown, gelatinous purée sold as laverbread. It is then rolled in fine oatmeal, shaped into cakes and fried using bacon fat, then eaten for breakfast. I have tried it and found the taste quite acceptable. Caerphilly cheese is found country-wide nowadays, mostly due to the fact that most of it is made in England and Ireland, but a few Welsh creameries still make this mild, moist, crumbly cheese.

Gloucestershire – famous for its Double Gloucester cheese, so called because it is made from the morning milk and some of the evening milk. Single Gloucester, extinct since 1945 is making a comeback and can be found at specialist cheese shops. Single Gloucester is made from the skimmed evening milk and does not need much ripening, unlike its double cousin.

Worcestershire – what else but Worcestershire sauce? Made to Lea & Perrin's secret recipe, it is very good for livening up tinned food, pies and tomato juice.

Rutland – this tiny county has recently been re-recognised, after a long campaign by its residents. The most famous products made here are those of the Ruddles brewery at Oakham, a must for all fans of Real Ale.

Leicestershire – home of Red Leicester cheese and Melton Mowbray pork pies. A real Melton Mowbray pie is notable not only for its design, but for the filling which is made from roughly chopped meat (not minced meat with extenders) and the layer of clear jelly around the meat, which is made from the concentrated stock of bones and rind. The outside crust should be crisp and brown.

Birmingham – like London is a melting pot of traditions and cultures. Fish and chip shops carry such tasty items as curry patties – these not only have a curried filling, but curry powder is added to the pastry, making them an attractive golden-yellow colour. If you've a sweet tooth, then a visit to an Asian sweet shop is a must, but don't buy too many of the confections on offer, they are very sweet indeed. Many of these shops can be found on the Stratford Road and while you're in that area, why not pay a visit to a Balti restaurant? Now hugely popular; if you like this kind of food, then you can still eat a very reasonable priced meal at a Balti house. Indigenous specialities include pork scratchings, pieces of pork rind fried until crunchy then seasoned. The best are sold loose in butcher's shops. Not for those with dentures or on a low cholesterol diet!

Staffordshire... look out for 'sandwiches' made with oat-cakes. These are not the small biscuit-like ones of Scotland, but a plate-sized flat bread made with oatmeal, full of holes like a crumpet. You can buy them at baker's shops and they are an ideal accompaniment to an English breakfast.

East Anglia... famous for Lavender and its fishing industry. You can't eat the Lavender, but the seafood can be very good indeed. Herrings, not as common as they once were, are made into bloaters. Sprats, crabs, mussels, whelks and cockles are widely found throughout the East Anglia coast.

Yorkshire – Sheffield Co-op shops carry a locally made sauce which looks like Worcestershire sauce but is sweetish and not even remotely hot. It goes by the name of Henderson's Relish; distinguished by its bright orange labels it is excellent with chips (in place of vinegar), mashed potato and stews. Yorkshire fish and chip shops have their own version of fishcakes; these are not pats of mashed potato with a hint of grey fish, but consist of a small piece of fish surrounded on two sides by slices of potato, then dipped in batter and deep fried. Additionally, haddock, not cod is what you'll get if you ask for fish. Cod has to be specially cooked to order. Coming from Yorkshire, I am perhaps a little biased, but I think that haddock is the better tasting fish. Tomato sausages, which are made of pork or beef with the addition of tomato purée and spices are a tasty change from the more usual sausage.

Lancashire – traditional home of Hotpot, Lobscouse and Wet Nellie (a kind of cake). Hotpot was once a fearsome mixture of salt meat, water and vinegar eaten with hard ship's biscuits. Nowadays it is the more familiar mutton and vegetables. Look out for miniature hot-pot pies on market stalls; in fact, markets in Lancashire are a good hunting ground for local specialities. Bury market in particular has a whole section devoted to black puddings, many of which will be award-winning. Baker's shops are well worth visiting for Parkin. This sticky ginger cake made with oatmeal is found throughout the north and is sold by the pound.

Lake District – in this area, local food is a tourist attraction, and you should have no difficulty finding regional foods. However, beware of the prefix 'Cumbrian' which is applied with great generosity to some unlikely foods. 'Cumberland', however is usually a sign of authenticity and the wonderful Cumberland sausage is an example of this. Kendal Mint Cake is often bought as a souvenir, but I'm not sure this dentists' nightmare would have survived without its fierce promotion. Salmon, trout and char are local fish that can be found in many fishmongers and restaurants.

Scotland – justly famous for its salmon, you could also try venison. Although not easy to cook in caravan, as it needs long, slow, wet cooking, many restaurants serve this meat as standard; indeed, I found it quite strange when visiting an Indian restaurant in Glasgow to find venison tandoori, venison tikka and venison curries of every heat prominent on the menu. Fish are very popular in Scotland, especially smoked. Try Finnan haddock, kippers and Arbroath smokies. The latter are fairly easy to cook in a caravan, because they are heavily smoked and don't require cooking, just heating up. Put the fish under the grill to warm, then split it open, remove the backbone, spread the inside with butter, close, then return to the grill to re-heat.

Ireland – North or South, the food is wonderful, if a little artery clogging. Because of the isolation from the mainland, Ireland still has a wealth of local specialities which are very easily found. At the baker's buy soda farls, both white and wheaten, wheaten bread and potato farls. At the butcher's, sausages are without compare to their mainland counterparts, while white pudding can be fried and eaten with breakfast. In cafés and restaurants, portion sizes are huge and you will need a drink with which to wash them down. Guinness, of course is world famous, but nowhere else in the world does it taste the same as it does here – rich, creamy and not at all bitter. If you are ever in Donaghadee in County Down, be sure to pay a visit to the Copelands Hotel, Warren Road, (the coast road). The food is wonderful and the portion sizes so big it's best not to eat for a few hours before you go. Other Irish beers are well worth trying, although you may find the bitter sweeter than the mainland brew. Irish whiskey, if you like a drop of the hard stuff is readily available and you will find many brands which are not exported. In the North, look out for Sullivan's, an apple brandy, which is advertised as 'legal poteen'.

Appendix 1

The Advantages of Canned Food

Many people think that canned food is not as good or as nutritious as fresh food; here is what the Canned Food Information Centre have to say on the subject:

- ✓ Only fresh and top quality foods are canned. No artificial preservatives are needed – canning and cooking preserve the food.

- ✓ Canned food is nutritious – many canned vegetables are even more nutritious than fresh or frozen versions. It is often low in sugar and in salt.

- ✓ Cans are simple to store, and do not need to be refrigerated, which saves energy and money.

- ✓ Canning makes a wide range of foods available all year round. Produce is harvested at its natural time, so there is no increase in price for food out of season.

- ✓ There is no wastage with canned foods, so they are economical. Using canned foods saves time and effort in the kitchen, and washing up is kept to a minimum.

- ✓ Almost all food cans are made of steel and are therefore easily recyclable with the use of magnetic extraction equipment at local council depots, or at local Save-a-Can banks. All steel cans already contain approximately 25% recycled steel.

- ✓ Cans are the most tamper-proof form of packaging around. The can opener is fast becoming a thing of the past as the availability of easy-open-end food cans grow. Offering all the benefits of the traditional food can, these are even more convenient – simply push down the ring, pull back slowly and the can is open.

For further information on canned food and recipe ideas for the home, call the Canned Food Information Centre on their Freephone number 0800 243364 or write to them at:

154 Great Charles Street
Birmingham
B3 3HU

Appendix 2

Metric Equivalents

Metric	Equivalent oz	Exact metric equivalent
5 g	¼ oz	7.0 g
10 g	½ oz	14.1 g
25 g	1 oz	28.3 g
50 g	2 oz	56.6 g
75 g	3 oz	84.9 g
100 g	4 oz	13.2 g
125 g	5 oz	141.5 g
150 g	6 oz	169.8 g
175 g	7 oz	198.1 g
200 g	8 oz	227.0 g
225 g	9 oz	255.3 g
250 g	10 oz	283.0 g
275 g	11 oz	311.3 g
300 g	12 oz	340.0 g
325 g	13 oz	368.3 g
350 g	14 oz	396.6 g
375 g	15 oz	424.0 g
400 g	16 oz	454.0 g
1 kg	2 lb	908.0 g

Liquid Measurement

125 ml	¼ pt	142 ml
250 ml	½ pt	284 ml
375 ml	¾ pt	426 ml
500 ml	1 pt	568 ml
750 ml	½ pt	853 ml
1 litre	2 pt	1.13 litre

Miscellaneous

1 Teaspoon	5ml
1 Dessertspoon	10ml
1 Tablespoon	15ml
2 cm	1in

A standard coffee mug can be useful for measuring liquids; it holds around a third of a pint. It is advisable, when following a recipe, to use either the metric or the Imperial measurements, and not mix the two. However, as most ingredients in this book are ready packaged, it is not necessary to be too pedantic about this.

Index

Also of interest:

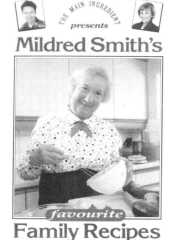

MILDRED SMITH'S FAVOURITE FAMILY RECIPES

Written by the much-loved star of Granada TV's "The Main Ingredient", this is packed with tempting recipes: everything from a simple (and foolproof) sauce to such treats as sticky tofffee pudding, banoffee pie and other sweets too nice to mention. Vegetarians are not neglected, with tasty recipes that the whole family will enjoy.

Published in association with **Granada Television**

£6.95.

We also publish a super range of outdoor and local heritage books.:

Lake District:

THE LAKELAND SUMMITS – Tim Synge *(£7.95)*

100 LAKE DISTRICT HILL WALKS – Gordon Brown *(£7.95)*

LAKELAND ROCKY RAMBLES: Geology beneath your feet – Bryan Lynas *(£9.95)*

FULL DAYS ON THE FELLS: Challenging Walks – Adrian Dixon *(£7.95)*

PUB WALKS IN THE LAKE DISTRICT – Neil Coates *(£6.95)*

LAKELAND WALKING, ON THE LEVEL – Norman Buckley *(£6.95)*

MOSTLY DOWNHILL: LEISURELY WALKS, LAKE DISTRICT – Alan Pears *(£6.95)*

Yorkshire:

YORKSHIRE: A WALK AROUND MY COUNTY – Tony Whittaker *(£7.95)*

YORKSHIRE DALES WALKING: On The Level – Norman Buckley *(£6.95)*

PUB WALKS IN THE YORKSHIRE DALES – Clive Price *(£6.95)*

PUB WALKS ON THE NORTH YORK MOORS & COAST – Stephen Rickerby *(£6.95)*

PUB WALKS IN THE YORKSHIRE WOLDS – Tony Whittaker *(£6.95)*

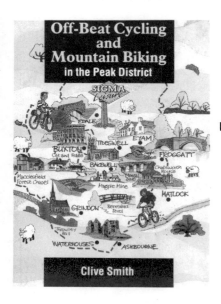

Cycling:

OFF-BEAT CYCLING IN THE PEAK DISTRICT – Clive Smith *(£6.95)*

MORE OFF-BEAT CYCLING IN THE PEAK DISTRICT – Clive Smith *(£6.95)*

CYCLING IN THE LAKE DISTRICT – John Wood *(£7.95)*

CYCLING IN LINCOLNSHIRE – Penny & Bill Howe *(£7.95)*

CYCLING IN NOTTINGHAMSHIRE – Penny & Bill Howe *(£7.95)*

– plus many more entertaining and educational books being regularly added to our list. All of our books are available from your local bookshop. In case of difficulty, or to obtain our complete catalogue, please contact:

Sigma Leisure, 1 South Oak Lane, Wilmslow, Cheshire SK9 6AR
Phone: 01625 – 531035   Fax: 01625 – 536800
E-mail: sigma.press@zetnet.co.uk

ACCESS and VISA orders welcome – call our friendly sales staff or use our 24 hour Answerphone service! Most orders are despatched on the day we receive your order – you could be enjoying our books in just a couple of days. Please add £2 p&p to all orders.